DOWNTOWN SUPER TELLS ALL

Poems & Lyrics

Dan Hubbs

The Troy Book Makers

Cover design by Mary Kathryn Jablonski
Cover Linocut "Sparkler Moon" by Rumara Jewett
Book design & format by Troy Book Makers

Typeset in Georgia, Tekton Pro Bold, Helvetica, Helvetica Neue Bold Condensed, and Gill Sans Bold

Printed in the United States of America
The Troy Book Makers • Troy, New York • thetroybookmakers.com

To order additional copies of this title, contact your favorite local bookstore or visit www.shoptbmbooks.com

ISBN: 978-1-61468-647-7

TABLE OF CONTENTS

ACKNOWLEDGEMENTS

I) IF YOU HAD THE MONEY

II) MOON TATOO & OTHER BANJO SONGS

III) WELCOME TO NEW YORK!

ABOUT THE AUTHOR

ACKNOWLEDGEMENTS

Grateful acknowledgement is made to these literary online sites where versions of these poems have appeared.

Mr. Beller's Neighborhood: *Ghosts, Sounds of the City, Spirit Ties, Water Bugs.*

Short Edition: *Slumgullion.*

The author also acknowledges and gives special thanks to

Todd Degarmo and the Folklife Center at Crandall Public Library
Mary Kathryn Jablonski, Poet and Editor
Rumara Jewett, Cover Art, Linocut "Sparkler Moon"
258 Broadway
Sheila Hubbs
Kitty Lindsey, Harborfields High School
Jean Callaci
John O'Connor and Seymour Barofsky
Pam Ratti
And most of all Michelle Hubbs

This publication is funded by a grant from the Alfred Z. Solomon Charitable Trust.

If You Had the Money

Spirit Ties

Because I sat around
Reading Joyce and
Wallace Stevens and
Shakespeare or spent
Time checking out
Museum shows and
Galleries and walking
Up and down the streets
Of the city, I had
A superior attitude
And even thought
I was hot shit
Compared to pawns
And poor assholes
Who had to wear
Suits and lug
Suitcases around
And sit in cubicles
But of course I was also
Just the Super, vacuuming
The hallway rugs
Mopping the lobby
At the tenant's beck
And call and I
Felt put upon
And embarrassed by
My lowly position on

The ladder of success
Being right near the
Financial district and
The World Trade Center
And all that. I was
Convinced I was an
Artist of some kind
And there's nothing
Better or higher
On a different ladder
Than that. I thought
A woman who was
A curator at the Whitney
Lived on the top floor
Of my building so
One day when I was
Tying off a bag
Of trash I was inspired
By those long industrial
Metal compactor trash
Bag ties and saw
That they looked like
Long spirits drifting
With the large loop end
As the head and the small
Loop end feet flowing
Out behind and I got
To work creating
A spirit world of
Garbage ties drifting

Tacked to a board
Down in the compactor
Room of the sub-basement
My studio where
I worked away oblivious
To the smell except
When now and then
A bag of kitchen trash
Or cat litter came
Crashing down, I'd
Look up for a second
Then get back to
Work on my installation
Of lost garbage tie
Ghosts I almost
Believed would
One day
Be displayed
In the Whitney Museum
Of American Art.

Awww, Man

When you're a Super
They'll call you
Any time day
Or night
There's no escape, man
It was the old
Korean woman
This time
Her English wasn't
Too good
It was six o'clock
In the morning
And the phone rang
Man is up here
What's that? Man is up there?
On six floor is here in hall
Like with most jobs
There's no rule book
You can check to
See if this
Is something you're
Supposed to know
What the fuck to do
Or if you should
Just go
Hell that's not
My problem

Call the police
Lady
But of course
I just put on
My sneakers, pants
Walked down the hall
And took the elevator
Up to the sixth floor
Some of the other
Neighbors were
Peeking out
Their doors
He's down there!
At 258 Broadway
The hallway is really
Windy
Alright
I walked along
Made the turns
And came upon the guy
Lying on his back
Looking at
The ceiling
He wasn't real old
Like maybe 30
Had on a ripped
Sport coat
Like a professor
Who'd fallen
From grace

And his big shoes
Were beat up from
Trampin' the streets
Worn through to a hole
On one foot so you
Could see the skin
Peeking through
Hey man, I told him
You got to go
Awww, man, he said
Yeah, you got to go, man
He reached his hand
Up and I
Took it and pulled
Him to his feet
He looked around
He hadn't shaved in
A while
You could tell he
Wasn't real sure
Where on earth
He was
I had to help him along
He was stumbling
Into walls
Mumbling about
How tired he was
And about how
He was cold
I got him down

To the lobby ok
But then he
Sat down against the wall
And goes, *sorry my friend*
Just a bag of bones
I had to lift him
Up again
While leaning against
The door and kind of
Pull him out onto
The sidewalk
Where already some of
The Wall Street go-getters
With their shiny shoes
And brief cases were
Hurrying on down
To offices and meetings
And wheeling and
Dealing
And he kind of staggered
A few steps
And then fell in
With them
The tops of his shoes flapping
Like clown shoes
And headed on downtown
In the falling snow

Shoes of New York, 1980

Ramon told me to come
On up to his neighborhood
Up by Harlem and hang out
With his friends and all
That. Sure man I told him
Is it cool though? I mean no
One will start anything or
Anything like that? No man
He said it's cool we have some
White people up here too man
We call them ghosts — just
You know when you're on the
Train or the street don't
Look at anybody all right?
Yeah I said and really that's good
Advice in general for the subway
And if you follow it you get to
Really check out the shoes
Of New York and if you're like
Me keeping your eyes to the ground
Or if you do catch someone's eye
You both always look away
Fast but thinking about it I'd say
It is ok to take a longer look at
An attractive person once they're
Out of the car on the platform anyway
And the doors are closed and the

Train's moving and even hold
That quick gaze knowing what
It means — well you're probably
Wrong about that anyway man —
Before the train is back in the dark
And you're just looking out at
The wall close up or once it
Opens up graffiti like at the old
Worth Street Station the flashing
Movie frames or dream
Images of colorful cartoon
Letters and spray-painted secret
Messages above old bums wrapped
Up in cardboard and blankets as
You pass by you're not even sure
If you really saw it or not
Contemplating the black hip
Chinese style slip-on jobs or
Little girl sneakers one crossed
Over the toe of the other that
Disappear when the car goes dark or
Black gleaming Wall Street wing-
Tips, beat up Van Gogh work
Boots high-heeled purple old
Lady sandals and so on shoes
You never saw in stores or any
Where you'll think I wonder where
The fuck all these shoes come
From like who made them in
What desperate sweat shop and

Where in what far off corner of
The world and how did they come
Here like what transpired or
Had to go down so that they'd
All be together today heading
Up to Spanish Harlem
New York City on the #5
Lexington Line Express train

Billy's Panther

Billy asked me
if I wanted to
go and smoke
some cigarettes
he stole some from
his old man and I
said sure and
we ducked under the
hole in the fence at
the Crescent Club
and walked out across
the 10th hole
fairway along
the 16th and
back into the
woods where
he knew about
a tree fort and there
we climbed up and
looked around there
were just some golfers
teeing off on 17
we lit up and puffed
away.
He told me his father was
a zookeeper and
that he had a panther

as a pet and a monkey
and so on and I thought
that was pretty cool
I didn't want to
tell him that Sal
had said it wasn't
true and that his father
worked at a gas station
I went along with
the story
and puffed at
the cigarette and then
handed it back to
him and I'm getting
an alligator too
he told me.
*

Hard to believe
but there had been
a bat flying around
in our classroom
at Washington Drive
School and the custodian
caught the thing and
at the end of the day
gave it to Billy saying
I know you really like
animals. That's why
you get the bat.
And Billy's face
lit up as he took

the box he asked me
if I wanted to walk
home with him
and check out
the bat and I was jealous
thinking I really like
animals too how come
I don't get a bat?
But off we went walking
down Washington Drive
carrying the cardboard
box with the bat
fluttering around
in there every
once in a while.
*

It didn't go well
at his house.
We went into the basement
and Billy opened
the box and the bat
flapped around
the room a few times
checking it out
moving slowly
it seemed
through the air
then it lit on the furnace
and crawled into
a crack where
the chimney entered

the cinder block wall
and that was
the last we ever
saw of the bat.
Billy was heartbroken
but he still had
the panther.
What about
the panther I said
and the monkey?
Well the monkey
is back at the zoo today
but I can show you the panther.
Ok.
Got to keep him locked
up in my sister's room.
He opened the door
ever so slightly
so as not to disturb
the panther.
See? He said.
I tried to look
over his shoulder
but he quickly
closed the door.
Did you see it?
I don't think so.
Here try again.
But each time
he had to quickly close
the door so the panther

wouldn't escape
or get upset
or some such
reason but I
really wanted
to see it.
Did you see him
that time? Billy asked.
I think so, I said.
I think I saw him
run past.
Yeah, he said.
That was him.

*

When Billy's mother
came home
it was time for his
diabetes shot.
She had the needle
in her hand holding
it up to the light
to check the dose
when she told me
I should go.
Billy was in the
bathroom crying
waiting for the shot.

*

Next day was
Saturday. I
went up to Sal's

house.
He asked me
about the bat
and I told him
what happened
and how Billy
had shown me his panther
and was getting
an alligator
and that the monkey
was back at
the zoo with his father.
Naaw, Sal said,
you don't really
think he has
a panther do you?
Yeah, I said
I think he does,
I think I saw it.
Sal shrugged his
shoulders and said,
Want to play handball?
and I said, Yeah.
So we got on our
bikes and rode
On up to the school
to see who
was around and
to get up a game.

If Martin Eden Could Do It,
So Can I

The other dish washer
Was a grown man
A big lumbering
Oddball named
George who
Had a crew cut
With lines
Of skin on his
Scalp showing
Through and who
Talked kind of
Slow and kind of
Loud. The chef
Was always on
Him making
Him stay late
And clean
The bathrooms
And come in
On Saturday
Morning and
Cut the grass.
George said
To me,
I do what I
Can to make

The world better.
I really couldn't
See how what
He was doing
Was helping
The world in
Any way
Whatsoever
But I recall
He was reading
MARTIN EDEN
And said to me
On numerous
Occasions,
If Martin Eden
Can do it,
Well so can I!
He didn't last long
At the Continental
French Restaurant
I was told
The chef
Had to let him go.
I thought about
George years
Later when I
Read the book
About how Martin Eden
Tries to climb
Out of the lowest depths

Of society
To win the heart
Of a wealthy girl
And how he fails
And ends up
Jumping off
A boat and swimming
Down
Farther and farther
Down
Until even
When
His body panics
And makes him stop
And head back
To the surface
It's too late
So I have to think
That when I knew
Old George
He just hadn't
Gotten to that
Part of
The book
Or that part
Of his life.

Montague Island

No work again
We were just sort of
Floating around out in
Prince William Sound waiting
For the long liners to
Come in with fish when
The bosses, the red hats,
Decided we could have
A shore leave on
An uninhabited island
Where they figured
Nothing too terrible
Could happen no
One would quit
For instance
Or get into a drunken
Brawl so they
Anchored the ship
And ferried 20 or
30 of us to a beach
On Montague Island
Telling us not to run
If we were chased
By a bear. It was
A sunny May day
And I walked up a little
Hill by myself and

Looked out at
The water and the sea
Birds, Arctic turns hovering
Puffins speeding by.
The head of an otter
Appeared down in the harbor
And she started swimming
On her back
There was a patch
Of snow under
A tree that was
Crisscrossed with
Animal tracks
And I sat there
Thinking for some
Reason that I'd
Come back here
One day.
Later I walked down
To the beach where
Some of the workers
Were standing in
A circle. *It's the
Vertebra of a whale,*
One of the oilers said.
Picking it up,
*It's not real
Heavy.* It was
A cream-colored cylinder
With two wings. We

All moved in
Five or six of us
Gathered around just
A few feet from where
The waves were breaking
Hilario from Guadalajara, Mexico
Nigel from Leeds, England
Noboru from Japan
Betsy from Oakland, California
Mike from Oneonta, New York
And reached out
And touched it
The vertebra
Of a whale.

Face Decides to Throw
a Table into the Ocean

I'd just been reading
TWELFTH NIGHT in
My bunk on the AK #1
And then after drinking
Someone had mushrooms,
High fantastical is right,
Our ship mate
Nicknamed "Face"
Decided the thing to do
Was lift one of
The folding tables
Set up for staff
On the stern
And heave the thing up
Over his head
With a running jump
Throw it out into
The waters of
Shelikof Strait
And we were all just
Kind of dumbfounded
Laughing nervously
Looking around
To see if any bosses
Had seen and what
Would happen next

When that line
About love
Receiving as the sea
And then falling
Into abatement
And low price
Came to me
And I was thinking about that
As the red hats appeared
And Face was led away
While behind
The surprisingly
Calm waters
The notoriously stormy
Shelikof Strait
Rolled on
And on

Northern Lights

To think that it
Had been Face
Who'd been in
And out of jails
My fellow fish
Processing pan-
Slammer
Who told me he
Shot heroin every
New Year's Eve
With his brother
Face who'd
Hyperventilated
In fear when
We passed a cop
On a long straight
Road somewhere
South of Kluane Lake
Yukon Territory
Face who was tall
With a beard
And a red
Lion's mane of
Hair growing out
And who you'd
Be glad was your friend
Because he'd worked as

A bill collector in
Anchorage and you'd
Seen him
Get pissed at this
Or that and tell stories
Laughing about putting
A beating on guys
Who hadn't paid up —
Who crawled into
My tent late
One night
In a campground near
The Yukon River
To shake my foot
And say, *Hey man,*
Come out and look,
And I'd followed
On hands and knees
And then looked up
Where Face stood pointing
Into the sky
At the green curtains
That wavered and shimmered
In the dark
Saying, *Isn't that*
Amazing?

Leaving Alaska

There was a young
Dall sheep
Standing in the road
Face pulled the truck
Over and we watched
It amble along
And join its sibling
And mom on the hill
And go up into the rocks
There had been a fire
And the burnt timber
Stretched off among
Rolling fields of
Lupine in bloom
Black stumps and
Branches in contrast
With the purple flowers
We stood a few minutes
Outside the truck
The gravel Alcan Highway
Behind us
Not a car or truck or
Traveler in sight
No engine sounds
No buildings no
Planes just us
Looking up the hill for

The wild sheep or
In the other direction
Out across
The field of flowers
To the distant
Yukon mountains we
Acknowledged
Face and Jane and I
With the briefest
Look or raised eyebrow
The moment
Then got back
In the truck and
Started down the hill
Toward Kluane Lake
And Destruction Bay

The Literary Life: NYC 1982

I recall distinctly
The famous author
Standing over me
As I scraped the plaster
Off her bathroom floor
Left behind by
Workers renovating
The building
The first time I talked to her
She called me up
To express her
Indignation
About the bathroom
I felt I'd done
Something wrong
Like I was in trouble
With my mother
Like I'd messed up
My chores
Or something
So I hurried on up
To her apartment
And met the famous author
All apologies
I got my little bucket
And paint scraper
And she showed me in

And pointed down at
The white spots on
The tile floor
*

The real estate company
Manager had told me
That her latest novel
Was being turned into
A mini-series about
Rich girls at a boarding school
Ok, I said, and shrugged
*

She watched me as I
Scrubbed and scraped
She'd written a book
On bathroom decoration
She said, *This mess*
Is completely unacceptable.
Her husband she told me
Was so and so
The owner of kitchen and
Bathroom stores
In London
One thing I'd learned
Growing up was
Don't talk back to
The woman in charge
Be a good boy
Don't fuck around
That's the lesson for

Workers and
Poets
It's ok to look up
And smile every
Once in a while
Otherwise
Eyes down
Keep on scraping
*

The Keshcarrigan
Bookshop was right down
Warren Street on
West Broadway
The owner was
A friendly person
With a lyrical Irish
Accent
She'd smile when
I walked in
Sometimes she'd let me be
Sometimes she'd
Make conversation and talk
About books
And authors
In her tidy shop I felt
Removed from the crazy
City just to be there
In the quiet with
The second-hand and
New books

The sunlight and
Shadows on the floor
I bought a Frank O'Connor
Collection
TRAVELLER'S SAMPLES
I bought THE COLLECTED
WORKS OF JOHN
MILLINGTON SYNGE
I'd linger looking
Through this book
Or that
And what do you do?
She asked me one day.

> *I'm a Super up the street*
> *at 258 Broadway*
> *on the park.*

Yes, or course, she said. *But*
Do you write,
Are you a writer, as well?
I hesitated, but then
I told her, *Yeah,*

> *Here and there.*

Well, isn't that
Wonderful?

> *I don't know if it is.*

And what is it you're
Working on?

> *I'm... I'm working*
> *On a novel.*

Are you? she said.
And then

She said maybe the
Kindest thing anyone
Has ever said to me,
Well, aren't you brave!
*

I guess you could
Take that different ways
But for a few minutes
There
Stepping back out
Into the city everything
Seemed pretty good
The streets crowded with
Commuters hurrying
For the subway
And me going
The other way
The cars
Honking and jockeying
For position to be first
To the tunnels and the red
Sunset between the buildings
Down by the river and
Walking just to walk
And looking up
The shadow of
The World Trade Center
One on the other
And a few clouds
Colored by the sunset
Moving above

Studying the Art of Love

Before anyone had
Moved in at 258
Broadway and before
The rugs were put down
I could hear
My partner's
Work shoes clicking
On the cement
Hallway as she
Came to see me
In the Super's
Studio apartment
At that time we
Had an intimate
Easy sex life or
Sometimes even
A deeper erotic
Energy where
You get out
Of yourself and
Are willing to try
Things and share
That experience
Without shame but
For whatever reason
After a time it
All began to

Fade away
*

The real estate company
Had a group of guys
From Greece going through
Painting all
The apartments
They lived together
In the Bronx
Saving on rent
To send money
Home to their
Families
One morning
I was up on
The seventh floor
Vacuuming when
A door opened
And they pulled me inside
Dragged me over
To the windows saying,
See? You like it Supe? See?
Across the air shaft
A few stories down
A young woman
Was undressing
Five or Six
Of us were at
The windows watching
As she got into

Her shower and
Turned on the water
And as the steam
Rose she
Faded from sight
*

On the Alaskan #1
Fish Processor
Where I had a job
As a pan-slammer
Banging frozen blocks
Of black cod out
Of heavy metal pans
So they could be glazed
And boxed
The bosses wore red
Caps and the line
Between hourly worker
And salaried manager
Was clearly established
And understood but
One night on shore
Leave in Seward
I sat on a stool
Next to Louise in
The Yukon Bar
And drank and talked
And nervous lines of
Separation were set
Aside her red hat

Was on the bar next to
Shot glasses and
Cold bottles of Bud
And then the song
By Dire Straits
So Far Away
Came on the juke
Box and we danced
Arm in arm
Close together
Spinning around and
Other crew members
Were dancing near by
Smiling not
Worrying about
The fishing
The work hours
The future just dancing
In the Yukon Bar
Drinking and dancing
Together until
Way into the night

So You Want to Be in Pictures?

There was a guy living on
The second floor who'd sailed
His own boat from
His home in South Africa
He was a pretty
Cool guy who filmed
Commercials and MTV
Videos and had some
Wacky hip friends
Who hung out
In Harlem and were
Often drinking
Or doing lines
In the place and when
They'd hear me going by
Vacuuming the hall
Would crack the door
And invite me in for
A hit
One night we were
Drinking whiskey
Sitting around before
Going to see
The Eurythmics at
The Ritz and his one friend
Who later ended up in
Prison in India for

Trying to smuggle some kind
Of drug over land in
A Jeep
Said, *Man, I come to*
New York City expecting
Like orgies and wild shit
Going down and instead
It's a bunch of business
People and dirty movie
Joints and buttoned down
Boring who-knows-what-all.
And we all went up to the
Roof to smoke a joint
And take in the summer
Night air
You could get a faint
Taste of the Hudson River
Up there when the wind
Was right and the lights
Of the Brooklyn Bridge
And his girlfriend was spinning
Around with her arms out
Laughing she was so
Happy she said
To be in New York
*

At one point I
Decided I'd leave
Being a Super behind
And see about getting

Into the movie business
I called him up to
See what might be available
And he was like, *Yeah*
Man, a guy I know is doing
A shoot and I'll tell him
You can be a P.A. So
I was like, *Sure whatever.*
That is, *I'll do it.*
The movie business
Is pretty fucking hard
Man, at least for a
Production Assistant.
You were paid by
The day and
The day started at five a.m.
Driving around setting up lights
With some other guys who
Hoped to become famous
Actors and directors
I got to hail a cab for
Whoopi Goldberg
I saw a room full of nervous
Actresses waiting to
Audition for a part in
A soda commercial
And the director came over
To me and said, *What do you*
Do when you're not a P.A.?
And all I could think of

To say was, *I'm a Super.*
But I always kind of
Thought I should have said
I'm an actor or a writer
Or something — anyway
The day just went on and on
By eight that night I felt
I'd given the movies a try
And was done
My colleagues warned me
I'd never be hired again
if I bitched and
Moaned and I said,
You know, I fucking hope not
It looks like a mighty
Long way man from here
Up to famous director.
And later that night I was
Back at 258 Broadway
Back to square one
Running the garbage
Compactor
And dragging out
The trash

If You Had the Money

If you had the money this
would be a cool place to live,
she said.
We were walking from the track
down to free lunch at the church
on Circular Street.
We glanced over at
the Fifth Avenue
Saratoga Springs mansion.
Yeah, I told her,
but if you had the money
you could get like
a place on Lake George
with a boat
and then just come down here
once in a while. Even
so, she goes, *well*
if you had the money
you could have the boat on
Lake George
and then just go up there
when you felt like going
on the lake.
Yeah, I said, *right,*
and I was thinking I
always wanted a place
down in the city, too,

and how if you had
the money you could
spend some time
down there going
to concerts and
restaurants and
all that,
if you had the money.

Moon Tattoo &
Other Banjo Songs

Old Saratoga Waltz

Belly up boys with your cash in the air
Win place or show the devil may care
If we win it will be a big night on the town
If we lose we'll just throw the ticket stubs down

It's a dance that was done in the days that are lost
When your love still loved you with kisses so soft
A dance that was done in the days we've lost
The Old Saratoga Waltz

That's one way to check and see if you're still alive
Put down your money and let it all ride
It buys a few minutes to plan out the fun
You'll have if the horse hits at twenty to one

Too-Ra-Loo as the light declines
My darling love from the rare old times
And the dance we did in the days that are lost
The Old Saratoga Waltz

It's fun to come up and go out to the track
The things you've lost you can win them back
Well life's just a gamble who knows what to choose
But the more you win the more you'll have to lose

Too-Ra-Loo as the light declines
My darling love from the rare old times
The dance we did in the days we've lost
The Old Saratoga Waltz

We did the Saratoga Springs Waltz

Moon Tattoo

It was out in L.A.
And down by the sea
I let the strangest fellow
Tattoo me
And my love was there
Pretty as could be
Saying sit down
And do it
I want to see
So he wiped away the blood
Methodically
And cut this moon's face
On me

The moon tattoo
There's no phases to
The moon tattoo
It will always
Remind me of you

It was out on the spit
In Homer, A.K.
We lived in a boat
That was beached
And decayed
One night by candle
You read my palm

And said well
Something's wrong
So you fell in love
With a boat captain
And we hitched a ride
To Kodiak Island
With him but
There was no work
Down in the canneries
There just the dalliance
Of eagles, booze and despair
So we spent one last night
In an old motel
And on the airport runway
I wished you well

The moon tattoo... (refrain)

It was downtown Manhattan
In '83
I let a dreamland desire
Take hold of me
I locked a door
And watched a screen
Where the women were
Acting generously
Obscene
And in City Hall Park
White petals came down
And covered the bums

Asleep on the ground
And a black rolling
Henry Moore statue
In just spring
For me and you

The moon tattoo... (refrain)

Helpless Love

Love pouring out
From a hole in a pail
Put it back together
With a hammer and nail

Tell my boss
What my analyst said
The boy's heart's broke
He's got to stay in bed

Helpless love
Helpless love
Helpless, helpless, helpless love
Helpless love bound to fail
Put it back together
With a hammer and nail

Joe Brennan told me man
It's just as well
Romantic love
Like living hell

Put this in
Where the love ran out
Tadhg's poteen
And some Irish stout

Like my brothers
I'm a working man
I can't make you love me
With two strong hands

I'm looking in the mirror
While I dance and flail
I'm working on a building
In the rain and hail

All Folked Up

All messed up
A coat full of cares
Town to town
Selling our wares

Dragging a pack
I found in Tralee
A hat an old bum wore
In NYC

A sheet music love song
That's tattered and torn
A scarf a teen beauty
Is said to have worn

A lone wedding ring
Its partner long gone
An old time song
Called "Travelling On"

And all the harm
That ever I've done
Forgive me darling
My only one

All messed up
All folked up
All funked up
All screwed up

A few lost souls
Turn out for the show
And sway to the fiddle
And the old banjo

All messed up
A van filled with woe
Guitars mandolins
And cheap bongos

While We Were Boozing

The girl that I love got married they say
She married some rich guy out in L.A.
His old man's a millionaire up in Monterey
Well that's that anyway

Springtime came in and springtime went out
While we were boozing
The apple tree blossoms got blown all about
While we were boozing

The geese got together and headed down south
While we were boozing
A snowstorm blew up and half-buried the house
While we were boozing

They say the world is changing
Maybe it's true
But I loved you then
And darling I still do

The suits on Wall Street were hauling in cash
While we were boozing
The preacher was preaching the first would be last
While we were boozing

I looked out on the street
I thought I saw you go by
I ordered a round
With a tear in my eye

Everything is changing
I see it too
But I loved you once
And sweetheart I still do

Springtime came in and springtime went out
While we were boozing
The apple tree blossoms got blown all about
While we were boozing

Hubbsy Boys

Hubbsy Boys raised in the ashes
Never learned to court the maids
They'd sit there kind of staring
Pretty girls made them afraid

So hop up pretty girls
Don't be scared
Hop up and dance

Hubbsy boys left Tralee
In them awful famine days
When they got to New York City
They knelt in the street and prayed

Hubbsy boys liked their beer
They liked to pass the jug around
Why pronouncements in the bar room
Boys we're treading holy ground

Hubbsy boys picked some flowers
Worked hard but still were poor
Too ashamed to show affection
Left the flowers at your door

Ain't Going to Work

Stopped to smell the lilacs
Stayed right where I was
Planets and stars
Kept turning above

I'm going to stop trying
To tell you I'm right
I'll say you are
If you let me spend the night

But I ain't going to work no more
I ain't going to work
Don't tell me that's what it's all for
I ain't going to work

Climbed Black Mountain
In the spring after rain
For no reason
Just to see it again

High up on the mountain
Lonely ravens fly
One follows the other
Just like you and I

I ain't going to work no more...

Honey I ain't never
Gonna be an entrepreneur
But I got a business deal for you
Here on the floor

My shack is on Black Mountain
It suits me fine
All I need is your lovely
Strange love valentine

But I ain't going to work no more

Nobody There

I hitchhiked to London
At nineteen years old
There was nobody there
In a city of gold

I wandered around Mérida
High on mushrooms
There was nobody there
At the Mayan ruins

I sailed out of Seward
Beneath an eagle in flight
There was nobody there
In a land without night

I stumbled round Dublin
Drunk as a lord
There was nobody there
In the land where my
Forefathers toiled

In a station of the Metro
Pale as a ghost
No one at all
For the one I love most

By the Russian River
I watched the salmon swim
Upstream to see
What was there for them

Windward Isles

I left Dublin and factory work
To sail before the mast
All them people troubling me
I told 'em, *kiss my ass*

I left school at an early age
To learn the stars and wind
I sailed with poets and drunkards and
thieves
And not one gentleman Jim

So damn your eyes
Captain Bligh
We're off to the sunny
Windward Isles

For many years I weathered the gale
I drank the siren's tears
At Five Points I lost all I had
After drinking ales and beers

Tahitian girls are a friendly lot
Just like the old sailors said
Unlike my darling Dublin girls
They're happy to take you to bed

So damn your eyes
Captain Bligh
We're off to the sunny
Windward Isles

We lost good men at Whytootackee
At Surabaya we lost more
The rum ran out in the Timor Sea
And the men all cursed and roared

And when the captain got out the lash
We gave him the old heave ho
We saluted his highness one and all
And watched as he sank below

So damn your eyes
Captain Bligh
We're off to the sunny
Windward Isles

The girl I love lives in Brandon Town
There by the Irish shore
I hope that I live long enough
To be with her once more

And when my shipmates have all passed on
To Fiddler's Green above
I'll stand on the dock with a toast of rum
And hail the life I've loved

Welcome to New York!

Welcome To New York!

When I was first
Hired as a Super
At 258 Broadway
NYC
I was the only one
Living in the
Eight-story building
The workmen who
Were converting
The place from an
Office building to co-ops
All packed up
And left in
The afternoon
So at night
It was just
Me walking
Up those long
Winding cement
Hallways
Half expecting
To see
Someone around
Each turn
Listening
To the sound
Of my own

Footsteps
Wandering through
The empty
Spaces that
Weren't apartments yet
Just big
Rooms that
Smelled like
Paint
And sheet rock
Plaster
The first floor
Had a big
Wrap-around window
On Broadway and
Down Warren Street
It had a high
Ceiling where
The discarded office
Desks and cabinets
And chairs were piled
Into a tangled mountain
That threw charcoal
Drawing patterns
Of shadows on-
The floor from
The streetlights outside
And I walked around
Carefully trying to
Be quiet and

Listen just in case
The off chance someone
Else was inside
The building with me
The elevator or
Pipes groaned or
Creaked on their
Own they whispered
To me up on
The eighth floor
I sat on a tool chest
And looked down
On City Hall Park
And across to
The Brooklyn Bridge where
The red taillights of
Cars drove out
And the white head lights
Of cars drove in
I sat and drank beer and
Pushed up the big
Heavy wooden windows
To let in the springtime air
It was my
Second night in my own
Big-ass house
So to speak when
The intercom buzzed
A friendly voice
Asked if I'd come

Down he just
Wanted to say hi
And welcome me
To the neighborhood
And I went on
Down a little
Skeptical and also kind
Of glad that someone
Even knew I was here
He shook my hand out
On the sidewalk
A thumb-to-thumb shake
That felt like I was
In on something
With him, he smiled
And said, *Hey man I*
Work in the neighborhood
Too, and so on, *but*
Know what man
I'm kind of stuck
I just need like five
Bucks to get out
To my family in
New Jersey I'm
Not bullshitting you
Man and I'll even
Leave my work shirt
See that's my name
Lou above the
Pocket that's me

I work right over
Here on Chambers
Man and if you can
Front me like five
Bucks I swear I'll
Bring you back ten
Tomorrow I'm
Not fucking with
You man honest to
God I lost my wallet
And just need some
Help you know
Man?
That shirt hung in my
Closet for a while
And then I started wearing
It around the building
When I was mopping
The floor or down
To the Raccoon Lodge
At night on Warren Street
So that some of the guys-
I knew used to look up
And smile when I came
Walking in for a beer
And say, *Hey*
What's up
Lou?

Water Bugs

Before I was a Super
If you asked me what
A water bug was I'd of said,
One of those little things
That kind of runs on the top
Of ponds or quiet pools
On the sides of streams
But at 258 Broadway down
In the sub-basement where
I had to make my way through
The cavernous half-lit
Cement spaces to get to-
The garbage compactor we had
The kind of water bug that's really
An overgrown cockroach
You'd think you saw something
Moving in the shadows and sure
Enough a water bug was
Running up the wall
Those fucking things are fast man
It kind of creeps you out
The way they run willy-nilly
Zigzagging at high speeds and then
Disappear into a crack in the cement
Or a sliver around a pipe by the ceiling
And you'd start to go, Man I wonder
If there's like millions of them

Under the floor and in the walls
And the ceiling and shit just
Kind of waiting biding their time
I was always looking here
And there and always seeing them
Running or even worse just
Standing still antennas moving
Feeling the air getting ready to run
I had to go down there once or
Twice a day to check the garbage
Compactor and tie off the bags
Of garbage that grew and
Snaked out across the floor
You had to tie off
The garbage tube sections then wheel
The sections over to the freight elevator
The elevator was just
A rusting platform with a metal arch
That pushed open the flaps
Above on the sidewalk so you could
Wrestle and drag the trash
To the curb
That elevator was an ancient
Hydraulic job that was always dripping
And the bugs liked the dirt and the puddles and
The spilled trash where mice would chew lines
In the plastic to get at the rotting food
I wasn't too swift about how the adjustments
Worked you had to add water check a gauge
Pump in some air, this and that, I really

Didn't know what the fuck I was doing
So this one day I get on the elevator
With my garbage tubes and I pull
The chain to start the thing and everything's
Cool and all I start rising up into the dark
Of the shaft the bell's ringing above to warn
Pedestrians to stand clear and
I looked way up at the yellow line of light
Two floors up where the flaps didn't
Quite join when all of a sudden
The fucking thing slows
Hesitates and then takes off
Like a shot flying up into the dark and
Slamming into the trap doors flinging
Them open and arriving into the daylight
I kept going up into the air a few feet
Then landed back down and stood there
As if everything was ok — the bell had
Stopped a taxi was driving up Warren Street
A young woman with a brief case who was
Walking by smiled at me we had the briefest
Passing surprised shared smile and I was just
About to lean down and start to drag
The garbage over to the curb when I see something
Peeking out of the plastic and sure as
Shit there's a water bug emerging from
Inside the bag crawling up and out right
Where my hand is grabbing the tied-off end
And just then the elevator decides to drop
To fall

Back down the two stories into
The dark and as it fell I
Collapsed back against my will
Sprawled out on the plastic
Tubes of trash looking up
And heard myself going,
Ahhhhhhhh!
As the doors closed above and shut out
The daylight again
And even as I was falling
For all I knew to my death
I was thinking about that
Water bug
Scurrying on my clothes
On my skin
And basically just pissed off
That my last thought on earth
Would be about that fucking
Water bug

Girls! Girls! Girls!

My partner was an
Enthusiastic feminist
Who had me read
Susan Brownmiller's book
AGAINST OUR WILL
And wanted to wear
A permanent black armband
To protest the failure
Of the E.R.A.
She taught me a lot
And what can you say
In your defense
Except admit what
Is true and beg
Forgiveness but
You become
A little unsure about things
For instance
We were in the crosswalk
On Chambers Street and
This cab cuts through
The crowd of
Pedestrians and she
Hauls off and kicks
The car door and
Of course it skids
To a stop in the street

And the guy jumps out
Screaming
And she goes
Nose to nose
With the guy cursing
He's waving his hands
She's pointing a finger
In his face
In these circumstances
Your role as male
Of the partnership
Is somewhat uncertain
But the cab driver
Was really no match
For her so the fact
That I'd just stood there
Dumb
Worked out
What do you expect,
She asked,
I'm Sicilian.
Or this other time the women who'd
Bought the apartment
Next door had us
Over for dinner
The three ladies had
A lot to talk
About: the rottenness
Of men the unfairness
Of society the failure of

The E.R.A. and so on
And again what do
You do but nod in
Agreement
And keep your mouth
Shut
She wanted to hold
My hand when we
Were out in public
Strolling around Tribeca
And I came to dislike
The hand-holding and
Developed a paranoid
Response to what
I thought was
A couple's parade but
Also knew I was
Betraying her as I
Gently pulled my fingers
Free
*

If you walked down Broadway
At this time
And made the left on Ann Street
There was a yellow
Sign proclaiming:
Girls, Girls, Girls
But if you got the nerve to
Duck in there
It was just little

Coin operated booths
With short porn
Movies
And white-collar Wall Streeters
Milling about
It was a little awkward
Running into some of the gay guys
Who owned places at
258 Broadway
We'd nod ever so
Slightly in recognition of
Our failure or whatever
You want to call it
Quickly look away
I'd learned to avoid
The booths that had
Round holes cut in the walls
I wanted to be alone
With the seeming generosity
And startling eroticism
Of the women and
Images brought
Up from somewhere
In my mind
I didn't even know were
In there to
The screen where I
Watched and hoped
As a half-hearted
Afterthought they

Were paid enough
For their trouble
And hadn't been filmed
Against their will
Seka was the star
I liked her films best
She encouraged
A certain attachment
And even inspired me
To write a poem
A kind of creation myth
Seka Creates the World
Based on Hesiod's
Theogony about how
Chaos was first and she bore
The barren sea and so on
I had the idea
And a first line
Hurrying past the dirty videos
Displayed
In that awful smell of bleach
They used to clean
The floor I wondered if it was
Something I could share with my
Partner or anyone at all
Since I was proud of
The general idea of the poem
But when I stepped
Back into the sun
And my mind

Returned as I
Made my way down
To Battery Park
And then stood
Looking out at
The water I
Knew it was something
I'd need to hide and
Bury pretty deep and
Keep to myself
When something my
Partner said came
To my mind,
Marriage is bad for women,
She said, *there's too much*
They have to give up

The Truck

He couldn't remember much
At the end of his life,
My Dad.
He didn't know who
I was.
He'd wake up
Pointing at nothing.
He asked where
His mother was.
What? my mother asked.
She's been dead for years.
       No, he said,
       Pointing,
       She's waiting for me.
He'd mumble,
He'd whisper
Something and
Stare into space.
Well, we're going
To say a prayer now,
My mother said.
       Ok, said my dad.
Hail Mary...
And so on,
Now and at
The hour of our death,
Amen.
He looked over,

He was holding
My mother's hand,
  I don't like that
  Last part,
  He said.
We all laughed.
We watched his old face
Mouthing no words
His cloudy eyes,
Bones of
His hands
Pulling on
The sheets
Over and over,
Picking at the fabric
Like pulling weeds
Faster and faster,
Staring at
The spot by his leg.
  You took my truck,
  He said.
What? my mother asked.
You don't remember,
You were driving all
Over hell and creation.
Lucky you didn't kill
Someone.
  You did,
  He said,
  You took my truck.
I'm doing everything for

You, she told him.
>*You're not doing anything*
>*For me,*
>He said.

Yes, she said.
She started crying.
>*Here,* I told him,
>*We'll get you sitting up*
>*A bit better.*
>*You can watch*
>*The Yankees.*

Ok, he said.
I got my hands
Under his arms
And heaved him
Best I could
So he was sitting up
Almost straight.
I turned the TV on
And found the ballgame.
He leaned back
Into the pillow
As the Yankees
Came up to bat.
>*You took it,*
>He said.
>*My truck,*
>*You took*
>*My truck.*

My Mother and Yang Hsiu

I'd been reading
Yang Hsiu
In translation
And his poems
Of flowers and
Wine and springtime
And lost friends
And as I rode
The bike trail
Today I guess
That's why
I noticed
So many flowers
Along the way
Queen Anne's Lace
And purple thistle
Flowering raspberry
And more
White water lilies
And purple
Pickerel weed
At the pond
Where I stopped
And worried
About my mother
85 years old
Not feeling

Well living
Alone
During the pandemic
I tried not
To think of
Tomorrow or
The coming
Months
When a butterfly
A monarch caught
My eye and I
Watched her
Floating or
Turning sharply
Looking for
The right place
To hover
And settle down

A Book About Life

She came to the desk
Shy but composed
Determined maybe
Eleven years old
And said, *Hi*
Can you help me find a book?
> *Yeah, I can help you find a book*
> *What are you looking for?*
Well...
She looked down and
Pulled at the hair
Behind her ear
> *What kind of book do you need?*
I need...
I need a book about life,
She said.
> *Ok sure a book*
> *About life.*
And there's
Probably lots of books
Here about life, right?
> *Yeah.*
> *Is there a particular*
> *Thing that happened or*
> *A particular time of life?*
Yes.
> *Ok.*

Yes, the early part of life.
          Ok, I think I know
          What you mean.
I mean when life first starts.
A book about how life
First starts.
          Ok sure we have books
          About that,
          How life starts for people.
          Yup let's see I'm
          Just checking the
          Computer, yeah,
          Come this way.
Ok.
She followed me to
The stacks and I knelt
Down and pulled out
Some books on human
Sexuality, books for
Young people and
I put them
In her hands
Thanks, she said
And she walked
Over to the table
And sat down
To read
And I went back
To the desk
A little worried

For her
About what she'd
Be seeing and
And really
Pleased that
The library was
Here to help her
And that I was here
To help her
And that she had
The confidence
To come up
To the desk
And ask for
What she
Needed
And sorry
Too that the book
About life
Had to be so
So hard

Motorcycle Hoodlums

Everyone wanted to see
My new minibike
My Great Aunt
Had money and she
Foot the bill
For a very cool
Minibike chopper
But my Mom was like,
No way, you're not
Riding that thing
On the road.
I bugged the shit
Out of her,

> *C'mon*, I begged,
> *Just up to the*
> *School it's not*
> *Even far.*

And like that until
She finally cracked
And said, *Ok but*
You don't ride
On the road you
Hear me?

> *Ok.*

You push it until
You get up there.

> *Ok.*

No riding, promise me
Give me your word.
>   *I won't ride*
>   *On the road,* I said,
>   *I promise.*

*

So I'm pushing it along
And it's pretty fucking
Heavy pushing it up
The hill on Pierce
And Ricky Olstein
Is with me and he's
Going,
C'mon man
Just let me start it up.
>   *I can't,* I said,
>   *Gotta push it.*
He took his turn pushing
Until we were
On Jefferson where
There's a hill down
So we glided
A little and then
Ricky goes,
Oh c'mon, man
Just let me start it up,
She ain't gonna
Know.
This will take forever
>   So I go, *Alright*

Man pull the

Cord, and we start

And go putting along

Smiling laughing,

Whoowee!!

Make the turn

Up Taylor toward

Washington Drive

And then sure

As shit there's

A car riding along

Next to us beeping

I pull over and

There's my mother

With her window

Rolled down

Giving me the

Look that makes you

Shiver in fear

The look that says, *I'm*

Gonna skin you alive!

I sat there dumb

Ricky sat there dumb

And then my mother

Starts to cry

Tears are dripping down

Her cheeks and she

Says, *You*

Gave me your word

You promised me.

And then she drives away
*

> *Shit,* I said, *I better*
> *Head home.*

Why, says Ricky,
She didn't say you
Had to.
And I was like,

> *I guess you're right.*

So we start pushing again
The gears are turning
As the wheels turn
On the pavement
It's slow going and
Then we're at the
Store and Ricky goes,
C'mon man let's
Start it again.
So I looked around
I looked long and hard
Down the road
Then Ricky pulled
The cord and I revved the
Engine let up on
The clutch and
Got the thing going
Really flying
Up Lone Oak Drive
Made the turn
Up Oneonta Court

And arrived
At the school yard
The kids playing
Handball stopped
To watch us come
Zipping across the
Ball field and
And down on to
The basketball court
Triumphant

Slumgullion

My grandfather had
Disdain for all ethnic groups
Irish were Micks
Jews were Heebes
Germans were Dumb Dutchmen
Hispanics were Wetbacks
Blacks were _____
Polish were Polacks
Italians were Wops or
Guineas — he thought
All religions a money
Making scam he
Didn't like politicians
Although he seemed to
Like Margaret Thatcher
Because she was a
Tough old broad
But meeting anyone
Face to face
He was friendly enough and
Polite but pretty
Light on
The small talk and
Even though he ended
Up as a school janitor
He didn't like FDR
He shook his head

In disgust he
Sighed a lot deep
Sighs of despair caused
By the stupidity
Of all people and
The workings of
The world
*

My grandfather
Lived in Bed Sty
Brooklyn when
He was a kid
The census lists
The family as black
In 1900, 1905, 1910
1915 but by 1920
They'd moved to
A different part
Of Brooklyn and
Had become white
His father was
A cook on sailing ships
Lots of black cooks
Historically and then
The unions kept them
Out of other jobs
His mother was
A seamstress, *The old*
Man, my grandmother
Laughed, *was only in*

Town long enough
To knock up
The old lady
When my grandfather was
Born his father
Was in Palermo,
Sicily, *I don't think*
There was a port
In the world he
Didn't see, my
Grandfather told me.
His father had
Been shipwrecked
Twice once
Off the coast of Africa
And once off North
Carolina where he
Floated to shore
On the wreckage
While a champion
Swimmer on board
Drowned. This seemed
To say quite a lot
To my grandfather
*

Once I asked him
If his last name
Could be Irish
What? he asked
glaring at me.

It's English!
ENGLISH!
*

I guess I was
The only one
In the family interested in
Ethnic history
Because my skin
Was pretty dark
And I had curly
Hair like my grandfather
And growing up
Kids were always asking me,
Hubbs what are you
Jew?
      No.
Paisan?
      Huh?
Means Italian. Are
You Italian?
      No, not Italian.
Then what?
I didn't know
I'd get a kind
Of suspicious
Look
      My Grandmother is
      From Ireland,
      I'd say.
They'd give up

Shrug their
Shoulders
We'd go back
To playing
Handball
*

At some point
Someone told me
I must be Black Irish
      What's that?
      I asked.
From when the Spanish
Armada sank and
The Spanish sailors
Came to shore
In Ireland.
      Oh, I said.
But when I
Visited Ireland when I
Was 19 and met
My Grandmother's
Family and saw
That they were all
Fair skinned with light
Hair and my aunt
In Dublin kept asking
Me, *What's your*
Mother's last name?
What is it? Because you
Look like a Jew man

To me.
Had to conclude
That the dark skin
Came from
Somewhere else
*

My Grandfather worked
17 years at
The Jamaica Water
Supply Company
And all he would say
About it was
A guy doesn't like
The way you wear
Your hair and
You lose your job
Then he was
A plumber but
The drink took hold
Of him and my mother
Tells the story
Of having to sit with
Him while he screamed
And shook in pain
From the DTs and
Of when her mother
Got her up at night
As a little girl
And brought her
Downstairs to

See her father
Passed out in
His vomit and
Sleeping under
The dining room
Table and she said,
Look and see
There's your father
That you love so much
You see? You see
How he is?
*

I recall watching
Him make slumgullion
Hunched over the
Cutting board
Wearing his glasses
Cutting onions
He'd gotten the recipe
From his father
He said and
They ate it
A lot growing up
He was a skinny
Old man with
Only two teeth
And bent shaky
Hands scraping
Vegetables into
The pan

Of butter and
Yellow split peas
*

My grandparents
Retired to a broken
Down farmhouse
In the country where
He built rooms and
Fixed the plumbing
And added a porch that
Looked out over
West Laurens,
New York and
Built a two-car garage
And a large garden
He'd stopped drinking
After falling down and
Cracking bones one
New Year's Eve and
Being told by my
Grandmother she'd leave
If he ever touched
A drop again
I watched him
With interest
Hoeing weeds and
Singing to himself
I could just hear
His voice
From the woods

Where I waited
Wondering as
He leaned on
The hoe and
Looked out across
The valley or
Watched a hawk
Circling above
*

It was years
Later I looked
Up the census
Records showing
My great grandparents
Were born in Barbados
One of the islands
Where people from Africa were
Brought by the English
Gentry to work
As slaves
On sugar plantations

Five to Seven, Champ

After a few drunken debacles
On shore leave they wouldn't
Let us off the boat
There were no fish and so
No work and
We were moored right there
In Resurrection Bay and at
Night a bunch of us gathered at the rail
And stared in at the lights of Seward
Cursing and full of mutinous
Hatred but then the fish
Started hitting out in
Prince William Sound and we
Raced on down there and
Got to work unloading
The black cod off
The long liners
*

You'd get your rain gear
On and rubber boots and
Down you'd go into the holds
Of the boats that were packed
Solid with fish
You had to shove your whole
Arm right into the wall
Of fish and slide as many as you could
Down into the net of the brailer

Then the brailer would swing up
And hesitate for a few seconds
Dropping strands of fish
Slime back down on us
And then swing over to our processor
To be dumped and frozen and boxed
*

You had to lean right into
The packed pile of fish bodies and
Get a good arm-full get
A good deep lung-full of fish smell
And keep on heaving
Them and throwing them
Filling up the nets while
Up above the bosses in
Their red hats peered down
Watching to make sure you were
Working as fast as possible
But you were out of sight
Part of the time
Down in the depths of
The holds flinging fish
And every once in a while
You'd get to
Sit down right on a pile
Of half-frozen black cod
And catch your breath
*

Kiley and I were working
Side by side hour after endless

Hour unloading one boat
Then another and
Then another so
You got half-delirious slap
Happy from exhaustion
And the sickening smell
And the rocking of the boat
Kiley started throwing fish eyes
Up at the red hats or
Whoever was looking down from
The rail or we'd duel
Standing back-to-back
In the icy water pink
From fish blood
Walk five paces turn
And shoot flinging
Fish out of
Rubber gloves
Through the air and that's
When Randy the chief red hat
Started getting on us
Calling down, *Kiley, how many*
More brailers you got there?
Let's see, Kiley said
He looked the load over thoughtfully
Holding his gloved hands out
As if to measure, *I'd say five*
To seven, Champ.

      Five to seven to go?
Yup, five to seven, Boss.

*

Twenty minutes later Randy's face
Appeared again over the rail
Of the processing ship and called
Down and again Kiley measured
Thoughtfully, even taking off a glove
And rubbing his chin then called
Up, *Five to seven, Killer.*
　　　　Five to seven?
Five to seven.
　　　　You said that a while back, Kiley.
It can be tricky to figure, Boss. But yeah
five to seven, I'd say.
　　　　Ok.
And that's how it went
Through the June morning each
Time they called down as
Pissed off as they'd get they'd
Get the same answer,
Five to seven, Buddy Boy.
Five to seven, Handsome.
And then he'd say something to me
Like, *Unless they want to fucking come*
Down here and unload it themselves,
Right?
*

And at some point after
The day had changed from grey
Drizzle to bright sun
And we both just

Flopped down on a pile
Of fish and stared up the
Sky as a bald eagle
Glided by looking down
For fish scraps and Kiley
Who was a happy Fourth Avenue Anchorage
Bum when he wasn't working
Said, *You know something Hubbs? You're*
Going to miss Alaska when you go
Back to New York.
We lay there looking up
Watching the eagle come in
And out of view
And I said, *Yeah Kiley*
I think I will.

Sounds of the City

Not Philip Glass
The other guy
Called me up
Asking if I'd come
Check out something
In his apartment
Was making a noise
He was kind
Of a nervous
Guy
So I go, *Sure*
I'll come see.
Although I'm
Probably the least
Handy
Super ever to
Hold the job
In the history
Of New York City
And I was thinking of how
He'd called me when
A manhole cover
Had blown
On Warren Street
And there wasn't anything I
Could do about that
Or even explain why

The fucking things
Decide to fly into
The air now
And again
But also
How people
Seem to like to
Say, *He's actually*
Better than Philip
Glass! Like
They have
Some kind of
Insider info
But at the time I'd seen
Koyaanisqatsi
And listened to
Kronos play
Philip Glass
And I liked that
A lot
The drive
And ominous
Surprising changes
Of the music
But anyway
I went on up
And we stood
In his kitchen
Listening to
A high-pitched

Buzzing sound
And I saw that
The timer on his
Stove was pulled out
So I pushed it back
In and that
Was that
He laughed
He was really a nice guy
But I still remember
How when I first met him
He tried to
Explain to me
Who he was
By saying,
I record for
Deutsche Grammophon
Records.
And I said,
Oh!
Because what do
You say to that?
I'm the Super. I
mop the floor?
You know
What I mean?

Ghosts

My Super's studio
Apartment had one
Window it must
Have been ten feet tall
With blinds that
Reached up to the ceiling and
A wand you'd twist
To open or close them
The mice would climb
That long wand
And swing a bit
As they climbed
Stop for a second
Then scurry on up
And disappear into
The ceiling
An exterminator
Came once a month and
Sprayed for roaches
And dropped glue traps
Here and there
In the sub-basement
And the mice would
Get stuck fast
Their fur
Sunk in
The sticky chemicals

But they'd still be
Alive
Squeaking
And then what
Are you supposed to do?
With a live mouse
Stuck in a plastic
Glue trap?
*
For a while there
A guy showed up
And walked under my window
Every night
He wore a suit
And a hat
And carried a brief case
He'd walk from one crack
In the sidewalk
A certain precise number
Of steps
To another crack in
The sidewalk
Where he'd turn
With a kind of dramatic
Flair
And repeat his journey
Of maybe 50 steps
Over and over
Is he there?
My partner would ask

And looking down
I'd laugh and
Tell her, *Yeah,*
	He's doing his
	Thing. But
She wouldn't laugh
And then it wasn't
Funny
How hour after hour
He'd walk
Back and forth
On the south side
Of the sidewalk of
Warren Street
*

One night
My partner
Shook me awake
She was sitting up
In my sleeping loft
Pointing out at the wall
By the window
Do you see it?
She asked me,
You see it, right?
Bleary eyed I looked
I thought it would
Be a mouse but
Instead I saw
A cloud

Floating
A greenish cloud
Or mist in the room
Level with
The loft
It was moving
Slowly through the air
Tell me you see it,
She said

     I see it,
     I told her
What do you see?

     Jesus... it's like
     A cloud or something,
     I whispered
We watched it
For a time
Holding each other
Until we didn't see
It anymore
Then she said,
Don't forget that.
Don't forget that we really
saw it, Ok?

     Ok, I said, *I won't*
     Forget.
Promise?

     Yes, I told her,
     I promise.

A Lot of Money, Man

The front door
Never worked right
The buzzer wouldn't
Disconnect the latch
Or the latch wouldn't
Set so anyone could
Just push
The door open
And stroll on in
The locksmith was
A Puerto Rican guy
Who worked out of
A shop on West Broadway
He'd come up with his
Tools in a bucket
And work on the lock
And the latch
I'd hang out
To guard the door
As people streamed by
Mostly white-collar people
Headed to Wall Street
Man, they cheaped-out on this door
It's just crap, he said.
And what do they get for
These places?
       The top one that faces the park

Is the most expensive.
Yeah, what'd they get?
A hundred
And eighty grand, I told him.
No shit? he said.
Who has that kind
Of money?
Yeah, man, I don't know.
That's a lot of fucking
Money, man. And look at them
All hurrying around, all worried
And what for, you know it?
Yeah.
I mean, for that money you get
To look at the park, right? Like
I can't look at the park? I can
Go over and sit in the park
Whenever I feel like it.
Yeah, that's right, I said.
We watched the cabs
Driving down Broadway
As we contemplated these
Pronouncements
Two philosopher-
Poets the Thoreau
And Tu Fu
Of Tribeca
1982
*

At that time

There was a Henry
Moore statue
In City Hall Park
A beautiful black
Rolling bronze
Woman relaxing
In a circle of
Park benches
And under a cherry tree
And I'd sit
In the morning
And look at
The newspaper
With a cup of coffee
As the cherry blossoms
Came floating down
And stuck to
The wet surface
Of the statue
And on a bum
Sleeping curled up
In the ivy
And on me
As lucky as any
Wall Street banker
The Super of
The co-op at
258 Broadway

ABOUT THE AUTHOR

Dan Hubbs is a poet, songwriter, old time style banjo player, and a librarian. He has performed at Caffè Lena, Skidmore College (Solomon Northup Day) and at numerous venues in Saratoga Springs and the Adirondacks. He worked as a building super in Tribeca from 1981 to 1984.

Dan Hubbs plays two-finger banjo and writes songs that sound like they might have been favorites a hundred years ago.

> **— Sarah Craig, Executive Director Caffè Lena**